DREAM SCHEMES II

DREAM SCHEMES II

EXOTIC AIRLINER ART

STUART SPICER

Airlife
England

Acknowledgements

I am grateful to the following people and organisations for their assistance in the preparation of this book:

Steve Anisman, Gustavo D'Antiochia, Mike Axe, Steve Bradley, Keith Chia (Singapore Airlines), Exavia, Carlos Garcia, Marjorie Horner (Northwest Airlines), Martin Horlimann, Ian Malcolm, MilSlides, Daniel O'Connor (ANA), Javier Rodriguez, Catherine Rosec (Air France), Bobby Skirde and Simon Watson. I am also greatly indebted to Phil Spicer for proofreading and his assistance in the research for this book. My thanks are also extended to all the airlines and individuals whose work has been realised on the aircraft featured in this book, for without them it would not exist.

First published in the UK in 2001 by Airlife Publishing Ltd

British Library Cataloguing-in-Publication Data
   A catalogue record for this book
   is available from the British Library

ISBN 1 84037 229 X

Typeset by Rowland Phototypesetting Limited, Bury St Edmunds, Suffolk
Printed in China

Airlife Publishing Ltd
101 Longden Road, Shrewsbury, SY3 9EB, England
E-mail: airlife@airlifebooks.com
Website: www.airlifebooks.com

Academy Airlines

Academy Airlines is a small Georgia-based freighter airline flying out of Griffin. In 1994 one of its aircraft, a 1943 veteran Douglas DC-3 (C-47A), N130D, was decorated with animals for a TV series. Academy liked it so much that they decided to retain the artwork. Known as 'Animal Crackers', the design features different animals on each side of the fuselage. This side features an ape, rhinoceros, alligator, elephant, emu and tiger. Another DC-3, N143D, owned by the airline is named *Miss Ali Gator* after it was, allegedly, recovered from a Florida swamp. (*Exavia*)

Introduction

Since the early 1970s, when Braniff painted one of its aircraft in a design by the artist Alexander Calder, airlines have used their aircraft to fly in a whole range of non-standard colour schemes to highlight a wide spectrum of subjects and occasions. In those early days to see an aircraft in a special scheme was a rare event but in the 1980s and throughout the 1990s more and more airlines have taken the opportunity to paint one, or sometimes more, in a special scheme. Anniversaries, competitions, seasonal events, corporate advertising and even politics have all featured on aircraft in recent years and examples of all these groups are covered in this book. Advancements in the techniques used to decorate aircraft have led to the increased use of special schemes. Computer programs and adhesive film specially created for use on aircraft have assisted in producing the ever more elaborate designs that grace various aircraft. Since my first book, *Dream Schemes*, appeared from Airlife in 1997 there has been an upsurge in the number of airlines that are seeing the benefit of dressing up an aircraft, to the extent that I have not been able to include many aircraft that did not appear in a full special scheme. A few of the rarer schemes from the seventies and eighties have now been sourced and also appear in this volume. As we enter a new millennium I have no doubt that the increase in the appearance of special schemes will continue as airlines strive to seek publicity and brighten up our skies and airports.

Stuart Spicer

Aero Lloyd

The Germany-based sportswear manufacturer, Trigema, went further than most logojet sponsors by having not one, but three, aircraft painted in its colours. Above the large 'Trigema' titles along the fuselage, a slogan reads '*Deutschlands grosster T-shirt und Tennis Bekleidungs Hersteller*' (Germany's largest manufacturer of T-shirts and tennis wear). The first aircraft to appear, McDonnell Douglas MD-83, D-ALLE, was rolled out in mid-1987 and was followed in March 1998 by Airbus A321-231, D-ALAH. The third aircraft, another A321, D-ALAK, was delivered to the airline in April 1999. The airline's fleet of seventeen aircraft, a mix of MD-83, A320 and A321 models, flies scheduled and charter services to sixty destinations in Europe, the Mediterranean and the Canary Islands. (*Author's collection*)

Aero Peru

Aero Peru was founded in 1973 by the Peruvian government when it merged the airlines TANS and the air force-operated SATCO. The airline was privatised in 1983 when it was bought by Aeromexico and a consortium of Peruvian investors. In 1998 Delta Air Lines acquired a stake with a $50 million investment. On 14 March 1999 Aero Peru suspended operations and its ten aircraft (three Boeing 757s, four 737s and three 727s) were returned to their lessors. Debts of $174 million were reduced to $60 million within a week of the shut-down but despite attempts to restructure the airline, the decision was finally taken by the major creditors to liquidate its assets. In October 1998, the year of the airline's 25th anniversary, it acquired Boeing 737-236, OB-1711, from British Airways where it had flown as G-BKYC. With Aero Peru it appeared with its tail adorned with images found on the famous Nazca Plains of Peru. Following the airline's demise the aircraft joined the fleet of the American start-up airline, Access Air. (*Exavia*)

Aerolineas Argentinas

When the football World Cup Finals were held in France in 1998 Aerolineas Argentinas showed support for its national team by carrying additional markings on two of its aircraft. The aircraft involved, Boeing 747-287B, LV-MLP and 747-212B, LV-YPC, featured several footballers and titles which read, '*Aerolineas, en 98 Mas Argentina Que Nunca*' (Aerolineas, in 98 more Argentine than ever). Early reports erroneously suggested that another 747, LV-OPA, also carried the titles but it emerged later that observers had been misled by a computer-modified photograph. In June 1999 the airline became the first Latin American airline to operate the Airbus A340 when the first of twelve on order was delivered. Aerolineas Argentinas also flies the Airbus A310 and Boeing 737. (*Exavia*)

Air Canada

When the 1998 Winter Olympic Games were held in Nagano, Japan, Air Canada took the opportunity to support its national team by decorating an Airbus A340-313, C-FYLD, with words of encouragement. The port side of the aircraft featured a yellow-clad downhill skier and the call 'Go Canada Go', while the starboard side portrayed an ice-hockey goal minder and the slogan in French 'On Y Va Canada'. The scheme was worn throughout 1998 and into early 1999 when the aircraft returned to the paintshop. When it re-emerged it was wearing another special scheme highlighting the airline's membership of the Star Alliance group. Air Canada currently operates a fleet of seven A340s. (*Exavia*)

After the 1996 Olympic Games in Atlanta, Georgia, Air Canada applied a special livery to one of its Boeing 767-233ER aircraft, C-FBEG, in honour of the Canadian sprinter Donovan Bailey. Competing in the 100 metres, Bailey clocked a World Record time of 9.84 seconds and became the first Canadian to win a gold medal in the race since Percy Williams in 1928. Unveiled on 29 October 1996, the aircraft, named *The Spirit of Donovan Bailey*, featured a likeness of the sprinter on the rear of the aircraft and a gold stripe along the fuselage, symbolising his gold medal achievement. The title 'Running with the Best' appears in English on the starboard fuselage and in French on the port side. With the amalgamation of Canadian Airlines into Air Canada in January 2000, Air Canada's fleet of 767s increased to thirty-six aircraft. (*Author's collection*)

Air Europa

Air Europa was the result of a plan by British airline Air Europe, which aimed to establish a European trans-border airline by setting up fully owned subsidiaries or by taking shares in existing airlines. And so came about Air Europa in Spain and Air Europe Italy. Shareholdings in NFD (Nürnberger Flugdienst) and Norway Airways completed the set-up, collectively known as Airlines of Europe Group. Established in 1984, Air Europa did not start operations until 1 November 1993. Its principal operation provides inclusive-tour services between northern and western Europe and resorts in the Canaries and the Balearic Islands. Scheduled domestic flights and long-haul flights to North America and the Caribbean are also operated by a fleet of Boeing 737 and 767 aircraft. In April 1998 one of the company's Boeing 737s, EC-GEQ, was the first Spanish airliner to carry a commercial when it was rolled out wearing an advertisement for the Italian drink, Martini. (*Javier Rodriguez*)

Air France

For the 1998 Football World Cup, which was held in France, Air France, as official airline of the competition, decorated sixteen of its aircraft with footballers wearing shirts depicting the national flags of the nations taking part. The two designs, by Patrice Larue, comprised one showing a goalkeeper diving and the other a player shooting for goal. Both players were virtually prone in order to fit onto the fuselage. Larue chose four ethnic types, two white (one blonde, the other dark-haired), one African and one Oriental. The designs were then printed on a special film developed by 3M and certified for aviation use. The resulting giant stickers, measuring up to 21 metres by 4 metres, were then applied by a team of five people, with the process taking between ten and twelve hours per player. The first of these aircraft, an Airbus A320 and an A340, were rolled out on 23 March 1998 and all sixteen aircraft were in service by 10 April. Four types of aircraft were used, comprising one A310, ten A320s, two A340s and three Boeing 747s. The player is shown on the starboard side and the goalkeeper on the port. The complete list, with the player shown first, reads; **A310**, F-GEMD, Saudi Arabia/Nigeria; **A320**s, F-GFKH, Bulgaria/ Yugoslavia, F-GFKM, Norway/Germany, F-GFKO, England/Romania, F-GFKU, Holland/Italy, F-GGEA, Morocco/Tunisia, F-GGEF, Denmark/Iran, F-GHQC, Scotland/ France, F-GHQE, Belgium/Cameroon, F-GHQF, Chile/Croatia, F-GJVA, Austria/ Spain; **A340**s, F-GLZK, Colombia/Brazil, F-GLZL, South Africa/South Korea; **Boeing 747**s, F-BPVM, Mexico/USA, F-GETA, Paraguay/Jamaica and F-GEXA, Argentina/ Japan. For the record France won the competition. (*Air France* (*Footballer*), *SPA Photography* (*Goalkeeper*))

Air New Zealand

Air New Zealand made sure that it was well prepared for the new millennium when it unveiled a special 'Millennium' colour scheme at Christchurch on 29 March 1998. Designed by Air New Zealand's livery designer, Catherine Rezaei, the Boeing 737-33R, ZK-NGA, has a different design on each side, representing Australasian events in 2000, such as the *America*'s Cup (sailing) and the Sydney Olympics. This particular aircraft was originally planned to roll off the Boeing production line for Western Pacific as N968WP, and would no doubt have received a special scheme in WestPac's service. It would appear that this aircraft was destined to fly in special colours. On 28 March 1999 Air New Zealand became a member of the Star Alliance Group. The airline's schedules currently serve thirty destinations world-wide. (*Exavia*)

The All Blacks, New Zealand's Rugby Union Team, is one of the most powerful and successful teams in the sport. With the Rugby World Cup Finals in Wales pending, Air New Zealand decided to decorate its latest Boeing 747-419, ZK-NBW, with a giant billboard of the team's front row of Anton Oliver, Carl Hoeft and Kees Meeuws. Designed by Catherine Rezaei, the 11-metre-high by 26-metre-long graphic covered some 220 square metres on each side. Leaving New Zealand on 23 September 1999, the aircraft flew the team to London in preparation for the competition. The image was to remain on the aircraft throughout the World Cup, and for a further three months if the All Blacks won. Unfortunately they lost to France in the semi-final and the graphics were soon removed. Air New Zealand's domestic subsidiary, Air Nelson, applied an identical scheme to one of the thirteen Saab 340As in its fleet, ZK-NSK. (*SPA Photography*)

Air Ostrava

Air Ostrava was formed in Czechoslovakia, now the Czech Republic, in 1977 and operates scheduled passenger and cargo services in association with the Czech national carrier Czech Airlines. Originally called Air Vitkovice, Air Ostrava adopted its present name in 1994. The airline's fleet comprises three Saab 340A aircraft, two of which have received special schemes in recent years. The first of these, OK-PEP, appeared in May 1997 wearing billboard titles and an illustration of the latest Skoda car model, the Octavia. This aircraft had flown in special colours before, when it flew for the Swiss airline Crossair, as HB-AHD, and was decorated in a colour scheme celebrating Switzerland's 700th anniversary. In 1999, Skoda took the opportunity to promote another new model car with Air Ostrava. This time it was the Felicia model that was depicted on Saab 340A, OK-UFO, with a red saloon model on the starboard side and a silver estate on the port side. (*Author's collection*)

Air Sofia

The Bulgarian airline, Air Sofia, was formed in 1992 as a passenger-and-cargo operator serving destinations in Europe, Africa and the Middle East. Passenger flights utilise a single Antonov An-26, while a small fleet of six An-12s performs cargo duties. Two of these aircraft were given additional markings. The first, LZ-SFG, was decorated with musical instruments. Sadly, this aircraft was lost in an accident at Lajes, in the Azores, in February 1998. The second, LZ-SFK, still flies with various animals painted on its rear fuselage. They include a camel, a horse, a Dalmation dog, a lion, a bear and a zebra. The airline also carries out contract duties on behalf of the United Nations. First built in 1960, around 200 An-12s are still flying with some seventy different operators. The aircraft shown was built in 1962. (*Exavia*)

Alitalia

Alitalia's first logojet was rolled out in April 1997 to advertise the hazelnut chocolates, 'Baci'. The confectionery is marketed by Perugina, a Nestlé company, and was initially due to be worn for one year. This agreement was later extended for a further year. The aircraft selected, Boeing 747-243B, I-DEMF, wears a basic Alitalia scheme, but in silver instead of the normal green, along with about 150 silver stars on a dark-blue background. The colours are similar to the wrapping used on the chocolates. The inscription on the fuselage, '*Baci dall Italia, Baci da Alitalia*' translates into English as 'Kisses from Italy, kisses from Alitalia'. Alitalia currently operates eleven 747s. (*Author's collection*)

A second logojet was to follow one year later when the Italian jeweller, Bulgari, selected Alitalia to promote its latest watch, called 'Aluminium', on Boeing 747-243B, I-DEMS, for one year. The unveiling at Basle was to coincide with the Basle Clock, Watch and Jewellery Fair in April 1998. Like the Baci logojet, the Alitalia markings were in silver with the rest of the fuselage in a lighter shade of silver. An image of the watch was wrapped around the forward fuselage. Some 1,600 man-hours over twenty-five days went into the painting process and used 1,300 lb of paint. This aircraft and the Baci logojet have now both been painted back into Alitalia's normal colours. (*Exavia*)

Alitalia's third logojet, McDonnell Douglas MD-82, I-DAVZ, was rolled out at Rome–Fiumicino airport on 10 March 2000 wearing the colours of the McDonald's fast-food chain. Unlike the all-red Crossair example, which came to the end of its five-year agreement in May 2000, the Alitalia version has a red underside and a yellow nose. Alitalia's 'A' tail markings are in red and yellow instead of the normal green and red. A slogan along the fuselage reads '*McDonald's vola con Alitalia*' (McDonald's flies with Alitalia). Passengers flying on the aircraft, which operates on Alitalia's domestic routes only, are given special promotional offers with vouchers that can be exchanged in McDonald's restaurants. (*Author's collection*)

America West

America West is no stranger to the world of the special scheme, painting eight of its aircraft so far in a one-off paint job. The sixth aircraft to receive such treatment was Boeing 757-2S7, N904AW, which was rolled out at the airline's home base, Phoenix, Arizona, on 17 May 1996, in the colours of the locally based state baseball team, the Arizona Diamondbacks. The unveiling of the aircraft was unusual in that the team were still two years away from joining the Major League. America West is the official airline for the team. (*MilSlides*)

America West's seventh painted aircraft, rolled out on 15 December 1998, also promotes a sports team, the Arizona Cardinals. The airline has a four-year marketing agreement with the Phoenix-based football team, part of which offers a special package for fans travelling to away games. Known as the 'Follow the Home Town Team on the Home Town Airline' package, it includes air travel, ground transfers, hotels and tickets to the game. Two other aircraft carry schemes supporting sports teams, with Boeing 757-225, N907AW and Boeing 737-116, N708AW supporting the Phoenix Suns basketball team. (*Author's collection*)

American Airlines

The jet age came to commercial aviation on 2 May 1952 when a de Havilland DH-106 Comet 1, G-ALYP, flew BOAC's inaugural jet service between London and Johannesburg. Six years later the Boeing 707 went into commercial service when Pan American World Airways introduced the aircraft on its transatlantic service to Paris. American Airlines was not far behind when, on 25 January 1959, flight AA 2 flew from Los Angeles to New York. Forty years later American celebrated its entry into the jet age. A brand-new Boeing 757-223, N679AN, without markings, was delivered from the Boeing factory on 14 January 1999 to the airline's maintenance facility at Dallas/Fort Worth, Texas, where the 1959 'Astrojet' markings worn by the 707s were applied. From Dallas, where the 757 was rolled out on 22 January 1999, the aircraft transited to New York's John F. Kennedy airport in preparation for the 40th anniversary flight three days later. The airline's statisticians have calculated that during those forty years, AA jets have made 169,000 flights over the route, taking 23 million passengers between the two cities. American Airlines is now the second-largest airline in the world, with around 700 aircraft flying to more than 160 destinations. (*Exavia*)

American Trans Air

American Trans Air was founded in August 1973 to manage the Ambassadair Travel Club. Eight years later the company received its Common Air Carrier certificate, which allowed it to develop scheduled and charter services. One of its larger charter programmes involved the transportation of military personnel for the US Armed Forces during the Gulf War, which resulted in the movement of 108,000 personnel in 494 missions for Operation *Desert Storm*. Today the airline operates scheduled services to over twenty US cities as well as services to Mexico and Puerto Rico using a fifty-five-strong fleet of Boeing 727, Boeing 757 and Lockheed L1011 TriStar aircraft. In 1998 the airline celebrated its 25th anniversary and decorated Boeing 727-227, N772AT, in a party scheme. This was joined on 31 July when Boeing handed over a new 757-23N, N520AT, in an identical scheme. (*Author's collection*)

All Nippon Airways – Pocket Monsters

Following All Nippon Airways (ANA)'s successful campaigns with 'Snoopy' aircraft in 1996 and 1997, 1998 saw the appearance of two aircraft featuring characters from the 'Pokémon' or 'Pocket Monsters' cartoon. 'Pokémon' first appeared in 1996 as a computer game and has gone on to become a cartoon series and film, generating a $5 billion industry worldwide. The film, *The First Movie*, has become the most popular animated film in cinema history. One of the most popular attractions for 'Pokémon' fans has been the appearance of several aircraft adorned with 'Pokémon' characters. On 1 July 1998, ANA unveiled two aircraft, Boeing 747-481D, JA8965 and Boeing 767-381, JA8569, with each side of the aircraft portraying a few of the 151 'Pokémon', characters, including the bright yellow main character, Pikachu. Such was the immediate popularity of the aircraft that a second Boeing 767 was added three weeks later. In February 1999, a fourth example joined the ranks and was called the US version as it was to be used on ANA's North American network. This aircraft, Boeing 747-481, JA8962, was identical to its three stablemates apart from the airline's ANA titles which appeared on the tail. The port side features the following characters (from the nose); Clefairy, Pikachu, Togepi, Mew, Mewtwo and Snorlax, while the starboard side shows Jigglypuff, Pikachu, Psyduck, Squirtle and Bulbasaur.

In March 1999, ANA announced that 'Pokémon' would once again grace its aircraft but this time the airline ran a design contest, giving children between the ages of six and twelve a chance to create a design to coincide with the release of the new 'Pokémon' movie in Japan in the summer. The winning design featured a blue nose and tail with different characters from those of the previous year. On 20 June 1999, the winning design was rolled out at Osaka–Itsumi on Boeing 747-481D, JA8964, closely followed by two Boeing 767-381s, JA8288 and JA8357. (*Exavia*)

All Nippon Airways – Snoopy

Following the success of ANA's colourful aircraft *Marine Jumbo* and *Marine Jumbo Junior* in 1995, which celebrated its 500-millionth passenger, the airline produced another aircraft in a special scheme for the winter of 1996/7 to promote its services to the ski resort of Sapporo on the northern Japanese island of Hokkaido. 1996 saw the 25th anniversary of ANA's operation of ski tours to Hokkaido and was the fifteenth year that 'Snoopy' had been the campaign's mascot. The scheme featured the *Peanuts* cartoon character, 'Snoopy' and his friends in various skiing poses, and adorned the fuselage of Boeing 747-481D, JA8961, a 569-seat version used on the airline's domestic routes. The aircraft first flew with this scheme on 3 November 1996 and made its last flight on 6 May 1997, before reverting to its normal ANA colours. The exercise was repeated for the following winter with two aircraft receiving the 'Snoopy' treatment. This time, however, the stickers that graced the aircraft, Boeing 747-481D, JA8965 and 528-seat 747SR-81, JA8139, were much larger. (*Author's collection*)

Ansett Australia

When Ansett Australia was awarded the status of official airline of the 2000 Olympic Games over QANTAS, the national airline of Australia, the company set about promoting its position by painting not one, but eight aircraft, in various colour schemes in the period leading up to the event. The first aircraft to carry the 'Sydney 2000' titles was Airbus A320-211, VH-HYB, which was rolled out in 1997 in a scheme featuring a white forward fuselage which blended into dark blue towards the rear of the aircraft. In June 1997, a Boeing 747-312, VH-INJ, was also treated with the same scheme. This was worn until August 1999, when the aircraft was returned to Singapore Airlines at the end of its lease and was replaced by another Singapore Airlines 747, 9V-SMB,

which became VH-ANA and also had 'Sydney 2000' titles applied. This time, however, the colourful background was omitted. The third variation was given to Boeing 737-33A, VH-CZT, and featured the three mascots for the games, Syd, Millie and Olly. Syd, a platypus, was named after the host city and represents water. Millie, named after the millennium, is an echidna and represents the earth while Olly, a kookaburra, representing air, is named after the Olympics. Two other aircraft, Boeing 767-216ER, VH-RMM, and Airbus A320-211, VH-HYR, carry the titles 'Official Airline of the Sydney 2000 Olympic Games' and are the least decorated of the aircraft to receive special marks. The final variation was painted on Boeing 767-324ER, VH-BZF, and Airbus A320-211, VH-HYN, and showed an Olympic torch-bearer and the titles

'Olympic Torch Relay'. The first aircraft, VH-BZF, left Athens, Greece, in May carrying the Olympic Torch, which was mounted in a special cradle and strapped into a seat in Ansett's Business Class section. After arriving in Guam the torch was transferred to a Fokker F100 of the Australian airline Flight West and flown to Queenstown, New Zealand, where an Air New Zealand Boeing 737 took charge of the torch to fly it from Queenstown to Auckland. The final leg of the aerial relay was undertaken by the A320, VH-HYN, the second Ansett aircraft in 'Olympic Torch Relay' markings, which flew the torch from Auckland to the central Australian Ayers Rock Uluru Airport, arriving on 8 June. From here the torch began its overland relay, which concluded in Sydney on 15 September for the start of the games, after a journey lasting 100 days. (*Exavia*)

Arkia

Tel Aviv-based airline, Arkia Israeli Airlines, was formed in 1950 by El Al and Israel's labour federation, Histradut, as Arkia Inland Services, and is the country's second-largest airline after El Al. Initially operating domestic services, the airline also started charter services with aircraft leased from El Al. In 1980, El Al sold its share in the airline to the parent holding company. Today Arkia operates about ten Bombardier de Havilland Dash 7s plus three ATR 72s on domestic services, along with various smaller types. Boeing 737s and 757s operate Arkia's international charter operations. In 1996 and 1997 three of the Dash 7s received special schemes when 4X-AHI appeared in the blue and yellow colours of Visa Miles credit card. Club Hotel then took the opportunity to promote its services, with two further Dash 7s being given the logo treatment. Although both of these aircraft featured a fish, 4X-AHA appeared in blue, while 4X-AHC came out in this rather garish green and orange scheme. (*Simon Watson (Visa), (Club Hotel 4X-AHC), Author's collection (Club Hotel 4X-AHA)*)

Austrian Airlines

When Austria celebrated the country's 1,000th anniversary in 1996, the national airline, Austrian Airlines, responded by featuring twenty-four of its distinguished countrymen along the length of Airbus A321-111, OE-LBB. The idea came about because people often said that nobody famous ever came from Austria. The portraits were created on a special foil that can withstand the fluctuations of heat and pressure during flight and the effects of de-icing fluids used in winter. They are made up of 240 separate panels weighing 70 kilograms in total, and which took 320 hours to position. The aircraft was rolled out on 19 June 1996. The faces are, from nose to tail; Franz Grillparzer (poet), Karl Schranz (skier), Toni Sailer (skier), Billy Wilder (film director), Friedensreich Hundertwasser (architect and painter), Romy Schneider (actress), Thomas Muster (tennis player), Herbert von Karajan (conductor), Annemarie Moser-Proell (skier), Konrad Lorenz (behavioural scientist and animal sociologist), Andi Goldberger (ski-jumper), Oskar Werner (actor), Egon Schiele (painter), Sigmund Freud (doctor), Johann Strauss (composer), Bertha Freifrau von Suttner (author), Kaiserin Maria Theresa (Empress), Joseph Haydn (composer), Franz Schubert (composer), Kaiserin Elizabeth von Osterreich (Empress), Kaiser Franz Josef I (Emperor), Rudolf IV von Habsburg (Emperor), Walther von der Vogelweide (poet and singer) and Wolfgang Amadeus Mozart (composer). (*SPA Photography*)

When the 'Millennium' aircraft went into the paintshop to have its artwork removed early in 1999 it re-emerged in another special scheme. The composer Wolfgang Amadeus Mozart was replaced with another composer in a tribute to Johann Strauss. The gold image of Strauss, who was born in 1825, commemorated the centenary of his death in 1899. Originally a conductor, he gave up in 1872 to concentrate on writing operettas and waltzes. Among his more familiar works are *The Blue Danube* and *Tales from the Vienna Woods* which gained him the title of 'The Waltz King'. Austrian Airlines currently has six Airbus A321s in its fleet. (*Author's collection*)

Aviaco

Aviaco – Aviacion y Comercio SA – was formed in Bilbao on 18 February 1948 as an all-cargo charter airline using Bristol 170 freighters. The following year scheduled passenger services were introduced serving Madrid and Barcelona from Aviaco's Bilbao base before the network grew to include the Canaries and the Balearic Islands. During this time the de Havilland DH-114 Heron and Aviation Traders ATL.98 Carvair, a DC-4 conversion, joined the fleet before jets were introduced in the shape of the Sud Aviation Caravelle. Iberia eventually became a major shareholder and Aviaco was handed some of the Iberia routes. In 1999, Iberia took full control of Aviaco, and its fleet of around thirty aircraft, a mix of McDonnell Douglas DC-9-30s and MD-88s, was absorbed into the Iberia fleet. Three years earlier Aviaco applied stickers along the fuselage of several aircraft in the fleet as sponsor and official airline of 'Vuelta 96', Spain's premier cycling event. (*Javier Rodriguez*)

BASE Regional Airlines

BASE (Business Aviation Services Eindhoven) Business Airlines, based in the Dutch city of Eindhoven, was formed in 1985 and began operations in 1989. The name change to BASE Regional Airlines occurred in 1994, and in March 1999 the airline became the tenth franchise airline for British Airways. BASE's small fleet of two BAe Jetstream 31s, three Embraer EMB-120 Brasilias and a single Beech 1900D, operates scheduled services between Eindhoven, Birmingham, London, Manchester, Rotterdam and Zurich. With the airline's schedules centred on major business cities and therefore attracting businessmen as its main clientele, *The Economist* saw BASE as a good outlet for marketing its business magazine. In early 1998, BAe Jetstream 31, PH-KJB, was duly given an all-red makeover with *The Economist* titles on the nose and tail. The wording on the rear of the aircraft is BASE's marketing slogan and reads 'So Easy to Fly With'. The aircraft remained in the scheme for two years and is now painted in the British Airways 'Union Flag' house colours. (*MilSlides*)

Braathens

Since the late 1980s Braathens has painted one of its aircraft in a 'Sommerflyet' scheme to promote its seasonal fares. In 1997 there was a break with tradition and the usual 'Sommerflyet' gave way to a scheme celebrating the 1,000th anniversary of one of Braathens' destinations, Trondheim. The city was founded in 997 by Olav Tryggvason, King of the Haarfagre, and the aircraft carries his name below the cockpit. The chosen aircraft was Boeing 737-503, LN-BRJ, veteran of many of the 'Sommerflyet' and winter 'Olympiaflyet' schemes. The paintings depicted on the aircraft are the work of local children and are different on each side of the fuselage. In April 1998, Braathens introduced a new livery and with it dropped the word SAFE (South America and Far East) which had been part of the airline's name since it was formed in May 1946. (*Exavia* (*Port*), *Author's collection* (*Starboard*))

Braniff

Braniff Airlines was probably responsible for starting the trend for airlines to paint their aircraft in non-standard and eye-catching colours, with its innovative 'Flying Colours' scheme, which was introduced in 1965, each of its aircraft being painted in one of seven different colours. In 1973 Braniff unveiled an avant-garde scheme by the artist Alexander Calder on DC-8-62, N1805, featuring red, blue and yellow abstract artwork. Calder was called on again to produce a colour scheme to celebrate America's bicentenary in 1976. With four Boeing 727 models to work on, Calder painted each aircraft in a slightly different scheme to represent the red, white and blue of the US flag in motion. One of these models is displayed at the Frontiers of Flight Museum at Love Field, Dallas. The chosen design was unveiled on Boeing 727-291, N408BN, at San Francisco in December 1975, just in time for the celebrations. (*Author's collection*)

British Airways

The Royal British Legion is an organisation that safeguards the welfare, interests and memory of those who have served in the British armed forces. Formed in 1921 as a result of losses during the First World War, the charity receives a good proportion of its funds from the sale of Flanders poppies which are made by disabled members and worn to commemorate the loss of soldiers, sailors and airmen during military conflicts. Since 1996, British Airways has given its support to the cause by painting one of the company's aircraft for about six weeks to coincide with Remembrance Day, a day which culminates in a two-minute silence beginning at the eleventh hour of the eleventh day of the eleventh month, the time at which the First World War ended in 1919. The illustrations show the first aircraft to wear the poppy, Boeing 757-236, G-BIKC *Edinburgh Castle*, while the Boeing 737-4S3, G-BVNM, was the chosen aircraft for 1998. After the removal of the special markings the aircraft was put into one of British Airways' 'ethnic' tail schemes, wearing the Irish 'Colum' design. After much negative criticism of the 'World Image' tail designs, BA quietly dropped the scheme and this aircraft now wears the 'Union Flag' design being adopted across the fleet. (*Author (G-BIKC), SPA Photography (G-BVNM)*)

Another of British Airways' good causes is a Christmas flight to deliver gifts from the BA staff to deprived children. In 1994 a competition was run for children to 'Paint-a-Plane' on a Christmas theme. Each side of Boeing 737-236, G-BKYK, wore a different design and the aircraft took gifts to Romania. In 1996 a similar approach was adopted and the children of St Mary's School, Datchet, a village close to London–Heathrow airport, were asked to create a design for the aircraft. The winning design, known as the 'Runners Christmas Special', was applied to Boeing 737-436, G-DOCS, which flew presents on 24 December to orphaned children in Sofia, Bulgaria. (*Mike Axe*)

Caledonian Airways

What would Bruce Wayne say? Rolled out on 16 April 1999, a Caledonian Airbus A321-231, G-CVYG, temporarily masqueraded as a 'Batplane' to transport passengers from Manchester to Dusseldorf for a Batman convention. For the charter, the tail was dressed with an image of Batman against a yellow background. After returning to England the aircraft reverted to its normal tail, having worn the special artwork for just four days. Caledonian began life in 1961 as Caledonian Airways, before merging with British United Airways in 1971 to become British Caledonian Airways. British Airways took over the airline in 1988 and merged it with BA's charter airline, British Airtours, to become Caledonian Airways again. A final merger in March 2000 saw the Caledonian name, and golden lion tail, disappear when the airline merged with Flying Colours to become JMC Airlines. JMC is named after John Mason Cook, the son of Thomas Cook, who developed the concept of package holidays. (*Author's collection*)

Cathay Pacific

Hong Kong became a British colony in 1841 during the first Opium War, which was waged between Britain and China from 1839 to 1842 when Britain was trying to force China to open its ports to trade in opium. Opium from British India paid for Britain's imports from China, such as porcelain, silk and tea, then only obtainable in bulk from China. In 1898 a treaty was signed which gave Britain the colony on a 99-year lease. When this lease expired, at midnight on 30 June 1997, Hong Kong once again became part of China. To commemorate the occasion Cathay Pacific decorated one of its aircraft, Boeing 747-267B, VR-HIB, with a representation of the Hong Kong skyline. Following its painting at TAECO's Xiamen facility the aircraft was flown on 19 June 1997 to Hong Kong. Named *The Spirit of Hong Kong 97*, the aircraft was re-registered as B-HIB when Hong Kong took China's registration prefix. The Chinese characters on the fuselage spell 'Home'. (*SPA Photography*)

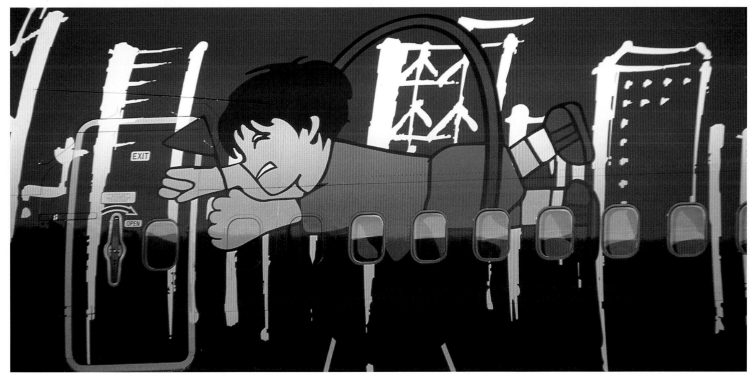

The Hong Kong skyline appeared on another of Cathay's aircraft shortly after the world celebrated the new millennium. In 1999 Cathay ran a design competition on the theme of 'The Spirit of Hong Kong into the New Millennium' and received over 3,000 entries. The winning entry, by a fifteen-year-old schoolgirl, Ho Sin Yee, from Hong Kong, featured a young athlete overcoming a series of obstacles to achieve his goal, set against a backdrop of the Hong Kong skyline. The slogan 'Same Team, Same Dream' appears in English on the port fuselage and in Chinese on the starboard side. The aircraft, Boeing 747-467, B-HOX, arrived in Hong Kong on 17 January 2000 after being painted at Xiamen. Cathay currently operates twenty-six 747s in its fleet of sixty-three aircraft. (*Author* (*Detail*),(*Nose, Port*); *SPA Photography* (*Full scheme*), (*Nose, Starboard*))

Cebu Pacific

Cebu Pacific Air was established in August 1988 but did not start flying until 8 March 1996. Based on the Philippine island of Cebu, the low-cost airline has certainly found a way to put fun into flying. All flights except early-morning departures are called 'Fun Flights' and passengers are encouraged to join in with Bingo, Name that Tune, Sing-me-a-Love-Song or Do-the-Demo (which gives the flight attendants a chance to act out their dreams). Prizes of baseball caps, mugs or free tickets give the games a competitive edge. Four of the airline's fleet of twelve McDonnell Douglas DC-9-32s, most of which came from Air Canada, are painted in schemes as wacky as the games played on the flights, and capture the energy of the Islands. RP-C1535, in a scheme representing a beach resort with sun, sea, sand and palm trees, was delivered on 30 November 1997 from Air Canada, where it was painted over five 18-hour days at Air Canada's Montreal maintenance base. In contrast, RP-C1536 wears a serious scheme celebrating the Philippine Centennial with '100 Years Kalayaan' titles. It was also an ex-Air Canada machine and joined Cebu on 24 October 1998. The last two specials also made the transition from Canada to Cebu with RP-C1509, named *City of Cebu*, in a scheme featuring the fish and music of the area, and RP-C1540, named *City of Davao*, in an orange scheme featuring local attractions such as the pineapple and durian. Cebu Pacific Air's tail logo is based on the country's Philippine Eagle. In mid-2000 the airline placed an order for ten Boeing 717 aircraft, plus four options, which will replace its fleet of DC-9s. (*Exavia* (*Tropical schemes*), *Author's collection* (*Kalayaan*))

Comair

Regional carrier Comair was formed in 1977 by father and son Raymond and David Mueller in Cincinnati, Ohio and started services the following year with a fleet of three Piper Navajos. Today it has grown to become the world's sixth-largest regional airline, operating 700 flights to eighty-one cities in the USA, Canada and the Bahamas. In 1984 Comair became a Delta Connection carrier and in October 1999 Delta took full ownership of the airline. It operates only two types, with Saab SF 340s and Swearingen SA-227 Metroliners being phased out in recent years as new aircraft have been delivered. Twenty or so Embraer EMB-120 Brasilias are by far outnumbered by the eighty-eight Bombardier Canadair Regional Jet 100s in the fleet, which make Comair the largest operator of the type. A further forty CRJ100 and 700 series aircraft are on order with options on another 110. In 1997 the airline celebrated its 20th anniversary and decorated CRJ-100ER, N979CA, which it dedicated to its then 3,200 employees. With the airline's growth it now employs some 4,500 staff. (*Author's collection*)

Compass Airlines

Compass Airlines started services in December 1990 following the deregulation of Australian domestic services the previous month. The airline initially operated two Airbus A300-600s leased from Monarch Airlines until its own A300-600s arrived. Two A310-300s were added in 1991 and flew until 20 December 1991, when the airline stopped flying because of difficult conditions created by Ansett and Australian, who did not welcome the new competition. In mid-1992 the company was resurrected when a new airline, Southern Cross Airways, was set up, taking over the assets of Compass. McDonnell Douglas MD-80s were leased in, but in spite of this the airline failed for the second time, and on 11 March 1993 it ceased flying once again. During its short life the airline saw two Christmases, and celebrated the 1992 festive season by applying appropriate markings to its aircraft. (*Author's collection*)

Condor

Condor Flugdienst is Germany's largest holiday airline, operating services to the Mediterranean, Asia, Africa, and North and South America. Established in 1955 as Deutsche Flugdienst, the airline started operations in March the following year with two Convair 440 Metropolitans and two Vickers Vikings. In 1961 the company's name changed to Condor Flugdienst and by 1965 jets were introduced with the Boeing 727. In the early seventies the airline became the first holiday charter airline to operate the Boeing 747. Later, the McDonnell Douglas DC-10 and Airbus A310 joined the fleet. Today, Condor operates a fleet of Airbus A320, Boeing 757 and 767 models and a single DC-10. In 1996 the airline celebrated its 40th anniversary and called on the services of the American artist James Rizzi to create a scheme for the occasion. His flamboyant design, known as the 'Rizzi Bird', was applied to Boeing 757-230, D-ABNF, which was rolled out on 28 March 1996 in its birthday colours. The aircraft was to fly in these markings for four years. Also in 1996, Condor placed an order making them the launch customer for the Boeing 757-300, which was some 23 feet 4 inches longer than the -200 series version and the longest single-aisle twinjet ever built. The first of twenty-four ordered was delivered in March 1999. (*Author's collection*)

Continental Airlines

Continental Airlines chose to see out the old millennium and see in the new with a flamboyant scheme created by the contemporary American artist Peter Max. Known as *NYC 2000*, the aircraft was rolled out at Newark Airport on 15 November 1999 in preparation for New York City's millennium celebrations. Painting freehand, two crews of sixteen worked twelve hours a day for eight days at Boeing's Everett plant and used 300 gallons of paint in the process. The nineteen colours used added 800 lb to the weight of the aircraft, some 300 lb more than is normally required to paint a Boeing 777. To bring the job into perspective, the 777's vital statistics may be useful: length; 209 ft 1 in, wingspan; 199 ft 11 in and height: 60 ft 9 in. The particular aircraft chosen, Boeing 777-224ER, N77014, is the last of an original order for fourteen 777s ordered by the airline. (*Exavia*)

Crossair

Switzerland-based airline, Crossair, is Europe's second-largest regional airline and operates a seventy-five-strong fleet with a mix of McDonnell Douglas MD-83, BAe/Avro RJ85 and RJ100, and Saab SF 340 and 2000 aircraft. The Saab 2000 was specifically designed for Crossair, which received thirty-four of the sixty-three aircraft built. Launched in May 1989, it made its first flight on 26 March 1992 and was named *Concordino* by Crossair, which received the first and last production aircraft. Number 59 off the production line, HB-IYD, appeared in November 1998, wearing a scheme supporting the Swiss bid to hold the 2006 Winter Olympic Games in Sion, in the canton of Valais. The design featured the Matterhorn on the tail and various winter sports and wildlife along the fuselage. Two other Saab 2000s in the Crossair fleet have also worn special schemes. The airline's twenty-fifth aircraft, HB-IZZ wears special '25th Concordino' titles, while another example, HB-IZK, found fame with its 'Phantom of the Opera' scheme. (*MilSlides, SPA Photography* (*Detail*))

EasyJet

The concept of cheap, no-frills airlines is an idea that has been working in America for over thirty years, but did not arrive in Europe until the mid 1990s. Luton-based easyJet was one of the first to adopt this method of operating, commencing schedules on 10 November 1995 with two orange and white Boeing 737-200s flying to Edinburgh and Glasgow. On 3 November 1997 Inverness was added to the schedule, and to promote the new service the local myth and attraction 'Nessie', the Loch Ness monster, was applied to the starboard side of Boeing 737-204Adv, G-BECG. This scheme was worn until late April 1997 when easyJet received its first -300 series aircraft and G-BECG went to Virgin Express. This aircraft and its start-up stablemate, G-BECH, now fly with the Argentinian airline LAPA (Lineas Aereas Privadas Argentinas). EasyJet currently operates fourteen -300 series aircraft and has thirty-two -700 series on order, with deliveries due between 2000 and 2004. (*Author*)

EasyJet has steadily grown since it began flying in November 1995 and, as new aircraft have arrived, so new destinations have been added to its schedules. The company's flamboyant chairman, Stelios Haji-Ioannou, has never been shy of publicity and has used his aircraft at every opportunity to promote a new service or air his views by applying a banner to his aircraft, often with a political message aimed at the local travel agents or a local airline. Greek travel agents were the target in July 1998 when a new service to Athens saw the slogan 'No Agents', in Greek letters, briefly applied on Boeing 737-3Y0 G-EZYC. Spanish agents were next, in September 1998, when *'Agencias de Viajes No'* appeared on G-EZYG. The following month British Airways was the target when easyJet objected to BA setting up its own low-cost airline, Go, arguing that the airline would unfairly subsidise its new franchise. G-EZYH appeared with 'Stop BA, Stop Go' on its port side only and still retains the markings some two years later. (*Author*)

In March 1998 easyJet acquired a 40 per cent stake in the Swiss airline TEA Switzerland and quickly took full control, renaming the airline easyJet Switzerland on 1 April 1999. Based at Geneva, this part of the easyJet empire has also received the banner treatment, with two aircraft appearing with unique markings during 1999. With easyJet's new Swiss hub, Boeing 737-33V, HB-III, appeared wearing *'Monopole Swissair, Non'* to let the national airline know that it would no longer have things its own way, while HB-IIJ promoted easyJet's Geneva –Barcelona service with *'Genève–Barcelone, toujours'*. (*Author*)

Germania

When Germania received its first Boeing 737-700, D-AGEM, at Berlin on 11 March 1998 the aircraft also claimed a world record. Leaving Seattle the day before, it broke the distance record in the 60,000–80,000 kg (132,675–176,366 lb) category by flying the 8,435 km (4,511 nm) in 9 hours 27 minutes. The pre-take-off weight of the aircraft was 62,248 kg (137,231 lb). The aircraft was also the first of three that the airline has painted in the colours of TUI, (Touristik Union International), Germany's largest tour operator. The other two aircraft are D-AGEN and D-AGEP seen below. Six other aircraft in Germania's fleet wear the colours of other tour operators and in 1999 these aircraft were leased to the airline LTU for five years. The six aircraft are D-AGEL and D-AGES (Jahn Reisen), D-AGEO (1-2-Fly), D-AGER (Tjaereborg Reisen), D-AGEV (Olimar Reisen) and D-AGEW (Meier's Weltreisen). D-AGEL has also worn another special scheme, when Boeing used the aircraft as its demonstrator for the 1997 Paris Air Show and world sales tour, wearing Boeing's 'Building on Success' colours. (*Author's collection*)

Gulf Air

Gulf Air, the national carrier of Bahrain, Oman, Qatar, and Abu Dhabi (UAE), celebrated its Golden Anniversary in 2000 by painting not one, but four, aircraft in celebratory schemes. Back in 1949 British aviator Freddie Bosworth took his seven-seat Avro Anson to Bahrain, where he gave sightseeing flights around the island. Local residents began to rely on his aircraft to commute between Bahrain, Doha and Dhahran, and on 24 March 1950, Bosworth, along with some local businessmen investors, registered the Gulf Aviation Company. Its first purchases included a de Havilland Dove and an Auster. Charter contracts with oil companies helped the early growth of the company. In the 1950s BOAC (British Overseas Airways Corporation) became a major shareholder in the airline, adding the Dove's larger stablemate, the Heron, to the fleet. Douglas DC-3s were also added to the fleet until the Fokker F27 replaced the older aircraft in 1968. In 1970 a BAC 1-11 was acquired and Gulf Aviation entered the jet age. The Vickers VC-10 was also introduced and destinations further afield such as London and Bombay were added to the airline's schedules. In 1973 the governments of the four countries purchased BOAC's shares and the airline was renamed Gulf Air. Three years later the Boeing 737 and Lockheed L1011 TriStar joined the fleet, followed by the Boeing 767 in 1988. Today the airline operates the Airbus A320, A330 and A340 alongside the Boeing 767, in its fleet of thirty-two aircraft, and these four types wear the '50th Anniversary' schemes.

The first aircraft to appear was Boeing 767-3P6ER, A40-GJ, which was unveiled on 28 March 2000 and was followed by A320-212, A40-EJ, on 2 May. The third aircraft, A340-312, A40-LD, was also rolled out in May, and the last of the quartet, A330-243, A40-KF, appeared in June. The artwork, which is different on all four aircraft, is the work of the Tunisian calligraphic artist Nja Mahdaoui, and is based on abstract Arabic calligraphy. Also on each aircraft is the '50th Anniversary' logo, which is inspired by the feathers of the Gulf Air falcon and which also combines the colours of the airline's three classes; red, maroon and green, with gold to symbolise the Golden Jubilee. (*Author's collection (A40-GJ), Exavia (A40-EJ), SPA Photography (A40-LD), (A40-KF)*)

Hainan Airlines

Hainan Airlines is a young airline, established in 1988 and commencing scheduled services in May 1993. Based on the island of Hainan, in the Gulf of Tonkin off the southern coast of China, the airline currently operates to over thirty destinations within China. In 1997 a new identity was unveiled and with it came the first of the special schemes that have since appeared on seven of the airline's seventeen Boeing 737-800s. Each aircraft depicts some of the tropical flora and fauna that are common to the Hainan region. Five aircraft each feature a local flower, with palm trees gracing another aircraft and a sea, beach and sun scene completing the set. In November 1999 the airline received the first of nineteen Fairchild Do 328JETs that are on order. (*Author's collection (B-2638), Exavia (B-2647)*)

Iberia

Iberia Airlines – Lineas Aéreas de Espana SA – had a difficult beginning. Founded in 1927 as Iberia Air Transport, the airline was forced to merge with a succession of others throughout the late 1920s and 1930s as the impact of the economic climate and the Spanish Civil War took its toll. The Second World War was soon to follow and in 1940 the government came to the rescue by acquiring a 51 per cent stake and giving the airline exclusive rights to Spanish air services. Following the war Iberia began an expansion programme that saw DC-3s, DC-4s and Lockheed Super Constellations in Iberia colours. In 1961 Douglas DC-8s became the first jets to join the airline and were soon accompanied by the Sud Aviation Caravelle. Today Iberia operates an all-jet fleet with a mixture of Boeing, Airbus and McDonnell Douglas variants. To celebrate the festive season of 1998 Iberia applied 'Feliz Navidad' markings to several aircraft including Boeing 747-256B, EC-DIA. (*Javier Rodriguez*)

Japan Airlines

When Japan Airlines celebrated the tenth anniversary of its Tokyo–Hakodate route in July 1999, the airline marked the occasion by applying a giant 15-metre by 6-metre portrait of the leading Japanese pop group GLAY. The four-man group hail from the city of Hakodate and JAL supported a special GLAY concert on 31 July as its official airline. Hakodate, a tourist and business destination, is situated on the northern Japanese island of Hokkaido. The aircraft chosen, a 563-seat Boeing 747-146B(SR/SUD), JA8170, flew from 1 to 15 July on the Tokyo–Sapporo route and then transferred to its Tokyo–Hakodate route until the end of August. (*Exavia*)

Japan Air System

On 1 September 1997, Japan saw the unveiling of its first airliner to wear an advertisement on its fuselage. Rolled out at Tokyo–Haneda domestic airport, Japan Air System Airbus A300B4-600R, JA8562, appeared in a blue and white scheme promoting 'Pocari Sweat', a high-energy sports drink produced by the Otsuka Pharmaceutical Company. The word 'Pocari' does not have any meaning but was created to sound cheerful and refreshing. Otsuka chose JAS to carry its brand name as the company was the airline's first in-flight advertiser, and the drink has been served on JAS's flights since 1980. The aircraft is pictured here taxying at Haneda in September 1998. (*Author*)

Prior to the 'Pocari Sweat' scheme another aircraft in the JAS fleet received a special scheme. Unveiled on 29 August 1995, McDonnell Douglas DC-10-30ER, JA8551, was rolled out at Tokyo–Haneda wearing characters from the Disney cartoon *Peter Pan*. Known as the 'JAS Peter Pan Flight', the aircraft flew charter flights, in a joint programme with the Kinki Nippon Tourist Company, from Japan to various locations including Hawaii, Australia, Bali and China over a six month period. At the same time funds were raised for the Peter Pan Children's Fund Japan, which helps seriously ill children. The first flight was operated on 2 September 1995 from Sendai, Japan to Honolulu, Hawaii. In March 2000 this aircraft left the JAS fleet and now operates with Northwest Airlines as N244NW. (*Exavia*)

Japan Asia Airways

Japan Asia Airways was formed in 1975 by Japan Airlines to fly its operations between Japan and Taiwan. This was to overcome any Chinese Communist objections to businesses that recognised the regime in Taiwan which may prevent the airline from operating to mainland China. Several other airlines have also created subsidiaries to avoid this problem, including British Airways, Swissair and KLM. Japan Asia Airways has added several other destinations over the years, including Bangkok and Hong Kong, which are flown with a fleet of four Boeing 747 and four Boeing 767 aircraft. In 1995 the airline reached its twentieth anniversary, and marked the occasion by painting ten Japanese dancing children on each side of Boeing 747-146, JA8128. (*Exavia*)

Linjeflyg

Linjeflyg was founded in April 1957 by Scandinavian Airlines System (SAS) and Aerotransport AB taking over the services of Airtaco, a newspaper and postal carrier. Initially using Douglas DC-3s, the airline progressed on to the larger Convair 440 before taking delivery of its first Fokker F28 in 1973. By this time the airline was operating domestic and charter services throughout Europe and by the late 1980s its

fleet had grown to twenty F28s. As the new decade arrived the Boeing 737-500 was introduced to replace the F28s. In 1986 one of these, SE-DGR, was given a full makeover with a landscape and titles declaring 'Sweden is Fantastic'. In 1993 the SAS Group was reorganised and Linjeflyg disappeared into SAS. The aircraft flies today with Air Botnia, a Finnish airline that was purchased by SAS in January 1998. (*Author's collection*)

Lufthansa

When Germany hosted its first ever World Exposition, 'Expo 2000', held from 1 June to 31 October 2000 in Hanover, the state capital of Niedersachsen (Lower Saxony), the organisers projected an attendance of some forty million visitors to the five-month long event, which showcases the cultures of 183 countries. Lufthansa, the sponsor airline for the event, played its part by painting one of its aircraft, Boeing 747-430, D-ABVK – appropriately named *Hannover* – in special markings promoting the spectacle. Four years earlier TAP Air Portugal painted one of its aircraft to promote 'Expo '98'. Lufthansa currently flies a total of thirty-four passenger-configured 747 aircraft made up of eight -200 series and twenty-six -400 series. On a typical transatlantic flight, a Boeing 747 will take on board about fifty thousand items including meals, drinks, headphones and blankets. Among the more unusual items in Lufthansa's emergency kit are a fishing rod, sunscreen and a copy of the Bible. Lufthansa currently flies to nearly 300 destinations in over ninety countries. (*Author's collection*)

In July 1994 Lufthansa became the first airline in the world to separate its passenger and cargo operations. With its main hub at Frankfurt, Lufthansa Cargo flies a fleet of ten Boeing 747-200Fs, nine McDonnell Douglas MD-11Fs and a single Airbus A300F4-200, to more than fifty countries world-wide. Illustrating its global operation, the airline painted a Boeing 747-230F, D-ABZF, with a special scheme showing its global freight network. Appearing in early 1998, the aircraft shows a series of clocks and destinations. The port side times and destinations read, from the nose; 08.00 Cologne, 08.00 Los Angeles, 13.00 Helsinki, 08.00 Singapore, Frankfurt on a world globe, 08.00 Chicago and 11.00 Madrid, while the starboard side shows 08.00 Bangkok, 13.00 London, 08.00 New York, 08.00 Stockholm, 08.00 Tokyo and 08.00 Hamburg. (*Author's collection*)

Lufthansa CityLine

Lufthansa CityLine, Europe's largest regional airline, started life in 1958 as Ostfriesische Lufttaxi (OLT), before becoming OLT Ostfriesische Luft-transport in 1970. Another name change occurred in 1974, this time to DLT (Deutsche Luftverkehrsgesellschaft). In 1978 DLT began operating a few services on behalf of Lufthansa which, in 1989, acquired a controlling interest in DLT, taking full control in 1992 and renaming the airline

Lufthansa CityLine. Today the airline operates to some twenty-seven countries and seventy-six destinations using a fleet of Bombardier Canadair CRJ100s and Avro RJ85s. Further examples of the CRJ100, plus the newer CRJ700 variant and Fairchild 728JET, are also on order. The Canadair CRJ100 was launched on 10 March 1989, made its first flight on 10 May 1991 and entered service with launch customer Lufthansa CityLine in November 1992. It was the airline's fiftieth jet, D-ACJH, that was chosen to help celebrate

its fortieth anniversary. Ten European landmarks, five on each side, representing the destinations served, were applied to the aircraft. The starboard side shows the Colosseum (Rome), the Eiffel Tower (Paris), Big Ben (London), Atomium (Brussels) and Cologne Cathedral, while the port side depicts the Little Mermaid (Copenhagen), the Leaning Tower of Pisa, the Brandenburg Gate (Berlin), the onion domes of eastern Europe, and the Prater (Vienna). (*Author's collection*)

Mexicana

In June 1997 Mexicana applied special 'Chivas' markings to its Boeing 727-264, XA-MEF, to celebrate the Guadalajara-based football team's success in a recent domestic cup competition. The Chivas team, which is sponsored by the airline, plays in red and white stripes. In 1990 Mexicana unveiled a new corporate image and applied eight different tail designs to its fleet, reflecting the country's traditions, culture, arts and crafts. However, in 1996 due to costs, the airline decided to reduce this to just one with the green and blue 'Nayarit' design, which is based on the Huichoi weavers of central Mexico. (*Author's collection*)

While most special schemes are applied to add some fun or colour to an airline's fleet, there are a few cases in which the application of a special livery has a more serious relevance. On 9 October 1997 the Pacific coast of Mexico was hit by the Category 5 Hurricane Pauline, which severely damaged the states of Oaxaca and Guerrero, including the coastal city of Acapulco. The government launched a relief effort and Mexicana supported this by flying food, drink, clothes and medical supplies into the stricken district. The aircraft used, Boeing 727-2K5(F), N909PG, was leased from the cargo airline Aeromexpress and painted with 'Puente Aereo Cruz Roja' (Air Bridge Red Cross) titles. The aircraft was returned to Aeromexpress on 28 October and the markings were removed. (*Exavia*)

Nationwide

South Africa-based Nationwide Airlines was established in 1991 and operates scheduled, charter and cargo services. The airline's fleet consists of Boeing 727, 737 and eleven BAC 1-11 aircraft, making it the second-largest operator of the type in the world. Its scheduled service to George, on the southern coast of South Africa, an area that attracts breeding whales, inspired the airline to paint one of its 1-11s, ZS-NUI, a -537GF model and one of the last to be built, in this striking whale scheme complete with barnacle-like grey patches of thick skin. The Right whale, which can weigh up to 60 tons, was once hunted for its blubber. As it was big and slow and floated once it had been harpooned, for the hunters it was the right whale to hunt, hence its name. Hunting of the Right whale has been outlawed since 1935. This particular aircraft, aptly named *The Right Whale*, previously flew with Cyprus Airways as 5B-DAH. (*African Aviation Slide Service*)

Northwest Airlines

On 15 July 1947, Northwest Airlines operated its first Pacific flight from Minneapolis to Manila, in the Philippines, on a journey that took thirty-nine hours to complete. Today, the same journey is made in under fourteen hours. In celebration of its 50th anniversary in 1997 Northwest decided to decorate an aircraft. A design contest was organised for children in nine US and ten Asia-Pacific cities to symbolise the culture of their homeland. Known as *The WorldPlane*, the winning designs from the nineteen markets were transferred into the largest decals ever made by 3M, and applied to Boeing 747-451, N670US. The aircraft entered service on 12 March 1997,

and flew in these markings until late 1998 when the aircraft reverted to its normal colours and was renamed *Alliance Spirit*. The main images on the right side of the aircraft featured Honolulu, the work of nine-year-old Thomas Robillard, which showed a boy playing a Ukulele. Ten-year-old Esther Johanna's image of Jakarta featured one of the dances of the local people. Seoul was represented by Ji Ah Chang's drawing of the traditional Mask Dance. The Beijing design, by Zhang Kun, showed a design called 'Building the Friendship Bridge'. Seven-year-old Akie Ohkubo drew Japanese carp streamers and Mount Fuji. Smaller designs represented San Francisco, Minneapolis/St Paul, Osaka, Memphis and Los Angeles. On the left side

of the aircraft eight-year-old Christen Capili's design was of children riding in a jeepney in Manila. Singapore's design, by Chee Xiu Xian, showed the Singaporeans in ethnic costume, the Merlion (a mythical beast, said to be half lion and half fish), the airport control tower and orchids. Kite-flying represented the culture of Bangkok as designed by Charinthorn Suriyaroj, and the final design showed the work of Christopher Ng's Hong Kong skyline within a Northwest aircraft. Other, smaller images showed Seattle, New York, Detroit and Chicago. For each of the winning entries Northwest donated $5,000 to the winner's nominated charity. (*Author's collection (Starboard), Exavia (Port)*)

Northwest's cargo division has also dressed up one of its aircraft to promote its transpacific cargo network. The chosen aircraft, Boeing 747-249F, N643NW, was delivered to Northwest on 15 July 1999, wearing the titles 'Investing in Pacific Trade' and the names of various Northwest Cargo destinations. The starboard side features the Far Eastern cities of Bangkok, Guam, Hong Kong, Manila, Osaka, Shanghai, Singapore, Taipei and Tokyo, while the port side of the aircraft displays the North American locations of Anchorage, Chicago, Detroit, Los Angeles, New York, San Franciso and Seattle. This particular aircraft was first delivered to the Flying Tiger Line in July 1980 and subsequently flew with Federal Express, Singapore Airlines, Northwest Airlines and Korean Air before being withdrawn from use in October 1998 and stored at Marana, Arizona. Northwest took it out of storage in May 1999 and prepared it for operations once more. Northwest now operates ten Boeing 747-200F variants in a cargo role. (*Exavia*)

Pacific Southwest Airlines

Pacific Southwest Airlines (PSA) was set up in 1945 in the southern Californian city of San Diego, and began services in May 1949 with a single Douglas DC-3 to Los Angeles. Other destinations within California followed as more DC-3s were added to the fleet. DC-4s and Lockheed Electras also joined the fleet before the Boeing 727 heralded the airline's introduction to jets in June 1965. The 737 was to follow in 1968, along with the Lockheed L1011 TriStar and BAe 146 in 1974. One of the airline's Boeing 727s, N555PS, appeared wearing titles wishing Walt Disney's Donald Duck a 'Happy 50th Birthday'. It is seen in front of an audience at Atlanta in June 1984. By the end of the year the airline had disposed of all its 727s as the McDonnell Douglas MD-81 and MD-82 joined the fleet. In the 1980s the US saw a frenzy of airline mergers and PSA fell victim to this when it was acquired by the US Air Group. On 9 April 1988, the airline was merged into USAir and the smile that graced the fleet of PSA disappeared. (*Author's collection*)

Pan Am Air Bridge

Chalk's Airlines was founded by Arthur Burns 'Pappy' Chalk in 1919. In its early days much of its traffic carried bootleggers to the Bahamas when the US Congress had ratified prohibition in the USA in January 1919. When prohibition ended in 1933 the airline turned its attentions to tourists and big-game fishermen. In the early 1970s Resorts International took control of the airline and renamed it Chalk's International Airline. After all, it did fly out of the USA, even if it was only fifty miles off the Florida coast to the Bahamas. It was then bought by a consortium and renamed Pan Am Air Bridge in March 1996. Air Alaska, formerly Wien Air Alaska, took a 70 per cent stake in the airline in early 1998 but collapsed soon after and forced Pam Am Air Bridge into Chapter 11 bankruptcy in February 1999. New owners were soon found in August 1999 and Chalk's International Airlines changed its name once more to Chalk's Ocean Airways. While operating with Pan Am Air Bridge in 1997 one of the airline's Grumman G-73 Turbo Mallards, N51151, was decked out in colourful livery promoting Corona Extra, a Mexican Beer. Built in 1949 as a Grumman G-73 Mallard, it was retrofitted with PT6A turboprops to Turbo Mallard status and is one of five operated by the airline. (*Author's collection*)

PLUNA

PLUNA – Primerias Lineas Uruguayas de Navegacion Aérea – was established in 1936 as a private company but was nationalised in 1951. In 1994, a 49 per cent stake was sold to a VARIG-led consortium, and from that airline in December 1997 PLUNA leased a Boeing 737-2Q8Adv, PP-VPD, to fly between the Uruguayan city of Punta del Este and Buenos Aires, the capital of Argentina. The rear of the fuselage was decorated with a design by the best plastic artist in Latin America, Carlos Paez Vilaro, who lives in Punta del Este. While with the airline the aircraft was re-registered CX-FAT. PLUNA's fleet currently stands at six Boeing 737s, which it uses on its South American services, plus one McDonnell Douglas DC-10 which flies the airline's Madrid service. (*Author's collection*)

QANTAS

Creating what was believed to be the first special scheme of the new millennium, QANTAS painted Boeing 747-438, VH-OJC, with a Formula One racing car along the fuselage in time for the first F1 race at Melbourne in March 2000. The scheme, designed by Cato Partners of Australia, also highlights QANTAS's role as official carrier for the Australian Grand Prix. The work was carried out by Aviation Exterior at Portland, Oregon before being flown to Australia. The aircraft was rolled out at Melbourne on 19 January 2000, displaying its generic F1 car which measures 22 metres in length and is 5.6 metres high. F1 flags are also worn on the upper fuselage. The car was hand-painted before being digitised on computer, then enlarged fifty times and transferred onto film. Thirty men worked for sixteen days to paint the whole aircraft, which involved a combination of fifty-two decals weighing 54 kilograms, and more than 800 litres of paint. The aircraft, appropriately named *City of Melbourne*, may be around for some time as QANTAS will have the official airline franchise for the next seven years. (*Exavia, Author (Detail)*)

Following the marketing success in 1994 of 'Wunala Dreaming', the design inspired by Aboriginal art used on its Boeing 747-438, VH-OJB, QANTAS again called on the expertise of the Balarinji Design Studio in Adelaide to create a design to mark the airline's 75th anniversary. The result, called 'Nalanji Dreaming', was applied to Boeing 747-338, VH-EBU, which was rolled out at Sydney on 16 November 1995 and celebrated the occasion with a special anniversary flight from Sydney back to its Queensland origins, overflying Winton, Longreach, Brisbane, and finally Sydney harbour before landing at Mascot airport. It entered service the next day by flying from Sydney to Tokyo–Narita airport. The aircraft is mainly used on the airline's Japan and New Zealand routes. 'Nalanji Dreaming', which means 'Our Place', depicts the blue and green colours of the tropical reef waters of the Great Barrier Reef and the rainforest of northern Queensland. QANTAS – Queensland and Northern Territory Aerial Service – was founded at Winton on 16 November 1920. (*Author's collection*)

Qualiflyer Group

The Swiss-led Qualiflyer Group was established in March 1998 and currently consists of twelve airlines; Air Europe, Air Littoral, AOM French Airlines, Crossair, Lauda Air, LOT Polish Airlines, PGA Portugalia Airlines, SABENA, Swissair, TAP Air Portugal, Turkish Airlines and Volare Airlines. The aim of the group is to establish a single high-quality standard among its members, with a degree of code-sharing and frequent-flyer programme integration. Several of the members have added the Qualiflyer logo and titles to a representative of their fleet, with AOM (Boeing 737, F-GINL), SABENA (Airbus A321, OO-SUC), Swissair (Airbus A321, HB-IOH) and TAP (Airbus A319, CS-TTG) all showing their alliance membership. Former member Austrian Airlines also applied Qualiflyer markings to an Airbus A320, OE-LBP, before leaving to join the Star Alliance group in April 2000. The AOM example is illustrated on a visit to Zurich in January 2000. (*Author*)

Ryanair

Ryanair was formed in early 1985 by brothers Cathal, Declan and Shane Ryan, commencing flights in July with a single Embraer Bandeirante operating from Waterford to London–Gatwick. The following year two HS 748s were added. Fares were kept low and frills were non-existent. By the end of 1986 a ROMBAC 1-11 was added after previously flying for the Romanian president. The acquisition of London European Airways saw the airline's fleet increase to six 1-11s and two ATR 42s. At this stage serious losses were being incurred until Tony Ryan, the brothers' father, injected millions of pounds into the company and the Irish government ended all competition on Irish routes for three years. The turbo-props were disposed of, the number of routes cut from twenty to four and by the end of 1991 Ryanair showed its first profit. The airline could once again begin expansion and in 1993 the Boeing 737-200 was introduced into Ryanair's fleet, which has since expanded to include twenty-one of the type. In March 1999 the first of a $2 billion order for twenty-five Next Generation 737-800s was delivered that will eventually see the -200 series aircraft phased out. An option for a further twenty 737-800s is also included in the deal. Ryanair has frequently added special markings to its aircraft to promote new routes or fares, or to celebrate a festive occasion, with Christmas giving an excuse to apply a festive message. One of the most colourful was the 1996 offering which featured a number of toys in addition to the normal Father Christmas face seen in earlier years. For Christmas 1997 one of a batch of six 737s acquired from Lufthansa appeared in an interim white fuselage with a festive bow and gift tag. Valentine's Day was also celebrated in February 1997, when EI-CKS was decorated in hearts, lips and Cupid and named *The Love Plane*. This is also the only aircraft in the fleet to carry 'Ryanair' titles in billboard form. (*MilSlides* (*Christmas 1996*), *Author* (*Christmas 1997*), *Author's collection* (*The Love Plane*))

Six of the -200 series aircraft have been painted to become very colourful logojets. The first to appear was EI-CJE in Jaguar Racing Green with a silver base and featured a 40-foot-long image of the Jaguar cat along the forward half of the fuselage. It was devised for the plane by Jaguar's Geoff Lawson and Fergus Pollock, the men responsible for Jaguar's XK8 model. Painted at FLS Aerospace Engineering's facility at Manchester, the aircraft was rolled out on 31 October 1996. Ryanair's second logojet was for the British daily newspaper *The Sun* and its Sunday partner the *News of the World*. *The Sun* takes the port side of the aircraft while the *News of the World* is featured on the starboard side. The aircraft, EI-CNT, previously flew with Lufthansa and joined Ryanair in December 1996. The next aircraft to carry an advert was EI-CNY, another ex-Lufthansa machine. Delivered to Ryanair in October 1997, the aircraft entered service the following month in the colours of the Irish beer Kilkenny. If you could tip the aircraft on its tail you would have your pint of beer, complete with creamy head. Number four in the logo stable was EI-CNX, which appeared in May 1998 advertising Tipperary Crystal. The badge on the nose promotes it as 'Ireland's Premier Crystal'. The most colourful of the logojets was rolled out at Southend in mid-November 1998 in a bright-blue and purple scheme applied by Air Livery. Carried by EI-CJD, the eye-catching scheme advertises Eircell, an Irish phone network, and features a mobile phone on the tail, complete with flying helmet and goggles. Ryanair's latest logojet scheme was applied to EI-CJC, which was rolled out at London–Stansted on 28 March 1999 wearing the bright-yellow corporate colours of Hertz Rent-a-Car. This aircraft was delivered to Britannia Airways in 1982, as G-BJCV, and flew with the airline until 1994 before joining Ryanair. (*Author* (*Jaguar*), (*Kilkenny*), (*Eircell*), *Author's collection* (News of the World), (*Hertz*), *SPA Photography* (The Sun), (*Tipperary Crystal*))

SABENA

SABENA, the national airline of Belgium, was founded in 1923 as Société Anonyme Belge d'Exploitation de la Navigation Aérienne. Services were initially developed to the Belgian Congo and expanded to Europe and North America after the Second World War. Today, SABENA's network encompasses over a hundred destinations in nearly fifty countries. The fleet comprises a mix of types, mainly from Airbus and Boeing. For twenty-four years SABENA flew five McDonnell Douglas DC-10s on its long-haul routes. These were disposed of but two more were leased pending the arrival of the Airbus A340 in the fleet. On 27 April 1997, the type was retired from the airline when DC-10-30, OO-SLG, operated its last service, arriving at Brussels from Chicago. An enthusiasts' charter was then flown before the aircraft departed for its new home in America with Continental Airlines. For those last few days, special markings were applied, advertising Disney's *101 Dalmatians* film on behalf of Belgacom, the official Belgian phone company (*Exavia*)

Singapore Airlines

When Singapore Airlines celebrated its Golden Anniversary in 1997 three of its aircraft were treated with a celebratory scheme featuring the '50th Anniversary' logo on the nose and golden wavy stripes running along the length of the fuselage. The company's history starts in 1947 when it was formed as Malayan Airways, initially flying Airspeed Consul aircraft and adding the DC-3, DC-4, Vickers Viscount, and Bristol Britannia to its fleet in the ensuing years, before entering the jet age in 1962 when the de Havilland DH-106 Comet joined the fleet. The following year the airline changed its name to Malaysian Airways and this was changed again in 1967 to Malaysian–Singapore Airlines. The present name was established on 28 January 1972 when the airline split into two, with each government taking control of its newly established national airline. Scheduled services started on 1 October 1972. Today the fleet comprises just four types, the Airbus A310 (which is being phased out), Airbus A340, Boeing 747 and Boeing 777. The three aircraft to be painted were Airbus A340-313, 9V-SJE, Boeing 747-212, 9V-SMZ and Boeing 777-212, 9V-SQA. (*Singapore Airlines*)

While it is important for an airline to have a respectable and up-to-date corporate image it is also vitally important that it attracts customers and fills the seats on its aircraft. So when Singapore Airlines dramatically changed its service with new levels of comfort, cuisine and in-flight entertainment in all classes, First Class, Raffles (Business) and Economy Class, the company needed to publicise the fact. Changes in First Class, for example, included reducing the number of seats from sixteen to twelve. In each mini-suite a personal 14-inch television screen and working desk now accompanied each seat-bed, and top chefs were brought in to create a new gastronomic experience. Having made these changes the airline set about promoting them by painting two of its 'Megatop' Boeing 747s in a flamboyant scheme called the 'Tropical Megatop'. The first aircraft, Boeing 747-412, 9V-SPK, was rolled out on 5 September 1998, at Changi Airport, with the second aircraft, 9V-SPL, following a few days later. This aircraft then departed at 09.00 on 13 September 1998, on a round-the-world flight, arriving at London–Heathrow before continuing on to Frankfurt, Osaka, New York and back to Singapore. The colour scheme represents a tropical beach and sky and also features a stylised 'FC', for First Class, a palm tree representing Raffles class and an 'E' for Economy on the fuselage. 'Now more than ever, a great way to fly' is written on the nose. Each aircraft took 2,500 man-hours and twenty days to complete, and used 560 litres of paint. (*Exavia*)

Skymark Airlines

Skymark Airlines is a new Japanese airline based in Tokyo that was launched to take advantage of the deregulated Japanese market. Operations started on 19 September 1998 with two Boeing 767-3Q8ERs on services between Tokyo and Fukuoka. Other destinations include Osaka and Sapporo. By spring 2001 the airline planned to operate international charter flights. The first aircraft, JA767A, arrived on 18 August 1998, direct from the Boeing factory where it had first flown ten days earlier. Once in Japan, markings were applied advertising DirecTV and showing a montage of sportsmen, musicians and TV studios. In March 2000 this aircraft returned to the paintshop, to re-emerge on 24 March 2000 in a new logojet scheme advertising the Yahoo! Japan internet site. The second 767 in the fleet, JA767B, was another new aircraft and made its first flight on 12 October 1998 before making its way to Japan, where it arrived on 27 October 1998. This, too, went straight to the paintshop and was rolled out promoting Microsoft and its Website. With two aircraft the airline was able to open two new routes, to Osaka and Sapporo. A third 767 joined the fleet during 2000. (*Exavia*)

South African Airways

One of the most colourful aircraft of all time is surely this Boeing 747-312 in the six colours of the South African flag. Over thirty-one days, a team of twenty paint technicians and workers painted the aircraft, using some 600 litres of paint in the process. South African Airways (SAA) commissioned the design company Red Nail to come up with a design and their abstract pattern depicting a 'cheers' symbol was inspired by a photograph of President Mandela celebrating the victory of Bafana Bafana in the football cup final in February 1996. Unveiled on 30 May 1996, the aircraft flew in time to take the South African athletics squad to Atlanta, Georgia, to participate in the Olympic Games one month later. Following the games the aircraft's 'Olympic' sticker was removed and replaced with a logo to promote the country's own Olympic bid for Cape Town 2004. Named *Ndizani*, which means 'to soar, to fly to new heights' the aircraft still retains the scheme as the airline enters the new millennium. (*Author's collection; SPA Photography (Nose)*)

In February 1998 SAA applied a special 'Valentine's Day' scheme to one of its Airbus A300B4s, ZS-SDC. Named *The Love Plane*, the entire fuselage was daubed with reproduction valentine cards and sponsors' stickers in aid of the Nelson Mandela Children's Fund. This scheme lasted only two weeks before the stickers were slowly removed, starting at the back of the aircraft and working towards the front. Eight A300s form part of the airline's fleet, which also includes the Airbus A320, and Boeing models 737, 767, 747 and 747SP. (*African Aviation Slide Service*)

South African Airways maintains a historic flight which includes a Douglas DC-3, Junkers Ju 52 (CASA 352L) and two ex-South African Air Force Douglas DC-4s, ZS-BMH (the final example built by Douglas) and ZS-AUB. ZS-BMH was delivered new to SAA on 9 August 1947 and was one of seven flown by the airline. In January 1966 the aircraft joined the South African Air Force and flew with 44 Squadron as 6904. On 12 March 1993 the SAAF handed the aircraft back to SAA.

ZS-AUB, named *Outenquia*, had a similar career. This was delivered to SAA on 10 May 1946 and flew with the airline until it too joined 44 Squadron in 1966 as 6905, before coming back to SAA to join its historic flight. In July 1998 'Happy Birthday Madiba' titles were applied to the fuselage of ZS-AUB. 'Madiba' is the nickname for Nelson Mandela and means 'Father' or 'Big Daddy'. (*African Aviation Slide Service*)

Southwest Airlines

Southwest Airlines is the largest low-cost airline in the world, with a fleet of more than 300 aircraft. The Boeing 737 is the only type operated, with a mix of -200, -300, -500 and -700 models. All of these aircraft wear a red heart on the fuselage to indicate that they achieved the number one position in the Department of Transportation Air Travel Consumer's Report for best on-time performance, best baggage handling and fewest customer complaints. This accolade was achieved for five consecutive years, from 1992 to 1996, and so the airline dedicated its eighth theme aircraft to celebrate the honour. This aircraft, Boeing 737-3H4, N647SW, was delivered from Boeing's Seattle factory on 9 June 1997 to the company's base at Dallas–Love Field. Named *Triple Crown One*, the aircraft features a large heart-shaped medallion draped over the fuselage. The 'Triple Crown' title is worn on the nose along with five hearts and the years 1992 to 1996 underneath. Southwest has dedicated this aircraft to all of its 24,000 employees and each one has their name listed on the overhead storage bin doors inside the aircraft. (*Author's collection*)

Southwest Airlines operates to over fifty destinations in twenty-nine states, with the majority located in western cities. In 1990 Southwest unveiled one of its aircraft wearing the state flag of Texas. This was followed in 1994 by an aircraft wearing the Arizona flag and, in 1995, a third was rolled out wearing the flag of California. On 20 May 1999, a fourth flag joined the airline when Boeing 737-7H4, N727SW, was delivered in the colours of the Nevada 'Battle Born' flag. More than 140 Next Generation 737-700s are on order and will join the fleet in the next few years. (*Exavia*)

In 1996 Southwest celebrated its 25th anniversary and, with several aircraft in the fleet already wearing special schemes, it was almost inevitable that the occasion would not pass without a similar treatment being afforded to another of its fleet. Boeing 737-3H4, N629SW, was delivered to the airline on 6 June 1996 wearing an all-metal fuselage with the Southwest colours and titles on the tail. Named *Silver One*, the aircraft's nose wore a stylised '25' forming the airline's familiar heart-shape. Four years later the scheme was revised to a matt silver fuselage as the all-metal one was perhaps too glaring in bright sunlight. Southwest started services on 16 June 1971 with three Boeing 737s operating between Dallas–Love Field, Houston–Hobby and San Antonio. Since those simple beginnings the airline has grown to operate a fleet of over 300 aircraft flying to fifty-five destinations. (*Author's collection*)

Star Alliance

The Star Alliance Group was launched on 14 May 1997 and brought together the global resources of the five founder members, Air Canada, Lufthansa, SAS, Thai Airways and United Airlines. VARIG joined the alliance five months later to become the sixth member, giving passengers access to over 600 destinations in 108 countries without the trouble of transferring to separate airlines on different sectors of their journey. The airlines benefited by being able to code-share on certain routes. These airlines each chose one aircraft in their fleet to receive a scheme showing their membership of the Star Alliance Group. Each aircraft was divided into six cross-sections, each wearing the titles and markings of a different member airline. This initially caused some confusion to those unfamiliar with the profile. The section nearest to the nose of the aircraft indicated its ownership. The airline's own tail scheme was replaced with a black tail featuring the five-triangle logo of the Star Alliance Group, representing the five continents of the world. SAS Boeing 767-383ER, OY-KDH, illustrates the style of presentation displayed by the early members. (*SPA Photography*)

By the end of October 1999 Air New Zealand, Ansett Australia and All Nippon Airways had joined the Star Alliance Group and it was All Nippon who initiated a new way of displaying membership on representative aircraft. The earlier wrap-around scheme was replaced with a box for each member draped over the top of the fuselage and down to the windows along its length. This style has been used by British Midland, Mexicana, Lauda Air, Austrian Airlines, Tyrolean Airways, and Singapore Airlines, whose membership brings the number of airlines in the Group to fifteen. With a combined fleet of 21,000 aircraft, over 800 destinations are now served in 130 countries by just under 10,000 daily flights. Tyrolean Fokker 70, OE-LFG, shows the style of presentation adopted by the recent members of the Alliance. (*Author*)

TAM

The Brazilian airline TAM (Transportes Aéreos Regionais), is a São Paulo-based airline and was formed on 12 May 1976, commencing operations exactly two months later. Its roots, however, can be traced back to 1962 and another TAM, Taxi-Aéreo Marilia, who, with VASP (Viaçao Aérea São Paulo), formed today's TAM to operate within the São Paulo state. Changes came soon after the 1976 formation and the fleet was upgraded and standardised with the Fokker F27. Ten years later the Fokker 100 joined the airline and in 1996 TAM was granted a licence for international flights. Once it was able to fly overseas TAM set about buying some new aircraft for the task and eventually Airbus were chosen to equip the airline for its longer routes. A forty-three aircraft order was placed, for a mix of A319, A320 and A330 variants, which are now being delivered. With this expansion TAM has become Brazil's second-largest airline. The airline has never been shy of dressing up an aircraft when the need arose, whether to blow its own trumpet for winning an award or celebrate a sporting or festive occasion. A few of the more colourful schemes are shown. In 1995 the airline was voted the 'World's Best Airline' by the magazine *Air Transport World*. When that happens, the airline wants to publicise it and so Fokker 100, PT-MRK, was suitably painted. In 1996 two more schemes appeared with Fokker 100, PT-MRX, wearing the colours of Brazil in celebration of TAM's 20th anniversary. Later in the year another Fokker 100, PT-MRD, was covered in gold stars for Christmas. Finally, for the 1998 World Cup football competition, the airline added 'I Love Brazil' titles and footballs to a Cessna Citation jet. Recently new routes have been introduced, to Paris and Miami, and titles appear on selected aircraft in the fleet to attract notice to this fact. (*Author's collection*)

TAP Air Portugal

TAP (Transportes Aéreos Portugueses) started operations on 19 September 1946, with DC-3s flying between Lisbon and Madrid. As the network expanded, so larger aircraft were added to the fleet, including the DC-4, Lockheed Super Constellation and Vickers Viscount. Jets joined the airline in 1962, when a Sud Aviation Caravelle was acquired. Boeing 707s and 727s were to follow. In 1978 the airline's name was changed to TAP Air Portugal. In late 1996 the airline painted one of its aircraft, Boeing 737-382, CS-TIB, in a special scheme promoting 'Expo '98', which was being held in Lisbon; with Portugal's history in exploration and discovery with early navigators such as Vasco da Gama and Ferdinand Magellan, the theme of 'The Oceans – a Heritage for the Future' was chosen. In May 1999 TAP's ten-year lease on the aircraft expired and it left to fly with Air Malta as 9H-ADM.

Early in 1997 another 737 in TAP's fleet, Boeing 737-382, CS-TIC, appeared in a scheme asking you to 'Fly Algarve'. Named 'Algarve', the scheme was based on the sea and sand, and also featured a rainbow along the length of the fuselage. Like its companion, CS-TIB, this aircraft's lease also ended in 1999 and it left to join the Mexican airline TAESA (Transportes Aéreos Ejecutivos SA). TAP now has just two 737s in its fleet, which also includes Airbus A310, A319, A320 and A340 variants. (*SPA Photography*)

Thai Airways

Since the thirteenth century royal barges have been seen on the canals and rivers of Thailand, known as Siam until 1939 (and from 1945 to 1949), and were used in waterborne state ceremonies. During the King's Golden Jubilee in 1996 a new barge was commissioned, called *Narai Song Suban Rama IX*, and presented to the King to sail in the Pha-Phra Kathin procession in which the royal presentation of robes is made to the monks. This joins three other royal barges, *Sri Suphannahong*, *Ananatanakharaj* and *Sri Sommeachai*, that have been used since 1782. It was *Sri Suphannahong* that was selected to grace Boeing 747-4D7, HS-TGJ, in a beautiful and ornate full-colour scheme. Unveiled in October 1999, the scheme features the barge with twenty-five oarsmen and the canopied royal throne, which is protected by royal sword-bearers and high-ranking officer guardsmen. The scheme is to promote 'Amazing Thailand', and is part of a two-year campaign to encourage foreign visitors to the country. A further enticement is a $179 multi-destination air ticket available to these visitors. With Thai celebrating its 40th anniversary in 2000, having begun scheduled flights on 1 May 1960, the airline decorated another aircraft in the fleet, Airbus A330-322, HS-TEJ, in an identical scheme. (*SPA Photography*)

100

The King's 72nd Celebration

HS-TMF

As well as Thai's two 'Suphannahong' aircraft, the rest of the fleet carried a birthday greeting to His Majesty King Bhumibol Adulyadej (Rama IX) on the occasion of his 72nd birthday, which fell on 5 December 1999. In Thai culture, twelve-year cycles are regarded in high esteem, with the sixth cycle being most significant. Born in 1927, the king succeeded to the throne after his brother's assassination in 1946. He is the world's longest-serving royal leader and is an accomplished musician, composer, photographer and sailor, spending up to eight months of each year in the countryside meeting officials and villagers to discuss rural development projects. (*Author*)

Trans Australian Airlines

Trans Australian Airlines started services on 12 February 1946 and was founded by the Australian National Airline Commission. Initial services were flown by Douglas DC-3s and, later, DC-4s, Convair 240s, Vickers Viscounts and Fokker F27s all flew with the airline. In 1964 the Boeing 727 introduced the airline to jet operations and was followed by the DC-9 in 1967. In 1980 one of each of these two types was painted in a special promotional scheme showing a couple on a palm-fringed beach.

Boeing 727-276, VH-TBK, also carried 'Central Australian' titles along the fuselage, while the smaller DC-9-32, VH-TJL, wore 'Coral Islander' titles. These colours were worn until 1983. In 1986 the airline changed its name to Australian Airlines and flew with this name until heavy financial losses in the late 1980s and early 1990s forced the government to merge the airline with another state-owned airline, QANTAS. The airlines were soon privatised and on 1 November 1993 the Australian Airlines fleet was integrated into that of QANTAS. (*Author's collection*)

Tyrolean Airways

Tyrolean Airways was established in 1958 as Aircraft Innsbruck and started services on 1 April 1980 with its present name. Over the years Austrian Airlines slowly increased its stake in the airline and took 100 per cent ownership in March 1998. Both airlines were originally partners in the Qualiflyer Group but switched their allegiance in March 2000, along with another Austrian airline, Lauda Air, to become members of the Star Alliance partnership. On 8 October 1998, Tyrolean unveiled one of its Bombardier Dash 8-300s, OE-LTD, in a special 'SOS Kinderdorf' scheme. SOS Kinderdorf (Children's Village) is a charity which offers a home to orphaned, abandoned or destitute children, and helps prepare them for the future. Founded in 1949, the charity now has 1,300 villages in 130 countries. The Dash 8, which will wear the scheme for two years, carries the legend *'Alle Kinder diese Welt sind unsere Kinder'* (All the children of the world are our children) on the engine nacelles. (*Exavia*)

UPS

UPS, United Parcel Service, is the largest package delivery operation in the world, with services to nearly 400 domestic and 200 international airports in 200 countries. On an average day 12.5 million packages and documents are delivered door-to-door. The company's operations started in 1981 using charter carriers but these were replaced when UPS started its own airline in 1988. In April 1997 passenger charters were offered to increase the utilisation of its fleet of over 220 aircraft. Five types currently make up the fleet, which consists of fifty-nine Boeing 727s, sixteen Boeing 747s, seventy-five Boeing 757s, thirty Boeing 767s and forty-nine McDonnell-Douglas DC-8s. Thirty Airbus A300-600s are also now joining the fleet. On 2 October 1998 UPS took delivery of a new Boeing 767-34AF, N320UP, with livery depicting match-stick athletes promoting the company as a sponsor of the 1998 Winter Olympic Games, held in Nagano, Japan, and the 2000 Summer Olympic Games in Sydney, Australia. A Boeing 757-24APF, N466UP, and 747-212B(F), N521UP, have received the same scheme. (*Author's collection*)

VARIG

Because Brazil is the most successful footballing country in the world, it is not surprising that the national airline, VARIG (Viaçao Aérea Rio-Gradense), has taken the opportunity, not once, but twice, to dress an aircraft up to flaunt its country's victories in the World Cup Finals. In 1994 a DC-10-30, PP-VMD, was given a green and yellow sash along with titles in Portuguese proclaiming 'World Champions of Football USA '94'. In 1996, in celebration of its 70th anniversary, VARIG introduced a new scheme to its fleet. The white was replaced by dark blue to represent VARIG's tradition as Brazil's principal airline. The compass rose was modified and coloured gold and yellow to suggest the warmth and brightness of Brazil's sunshine. When the World Cup came around in 1998 VARIG again painted an aircraft, celebrating Brazil's participation in the competition. The front of the aircraft, McDonnell Douglas MD-11, PP-VPP, displayed the badge of the Brazilian football team, while four stars represented their previous successes in the competition in 1958, 1962, 1970 and 1994. This time, however, they were unable to retain the trophy they had won four years earlier, the World Cup final being won by the home nation, France. A Boeing 737-3K9, PP-VOZ, was treated with an identical scheme. (*Author's collection*)

Virgin Atlantic Airways

The Virgin 'Scarlet Lady' is synonymous with the Virgin name and is proudly worn on the nose of every aircraft in the Virgin Atlantic fleet. Originally the lady was draped in a red cloak but, following British Airways' controversial decision to drop the Union Flag in favour of up to fifty ethnic tail designs, Virgin quickly stepped in and replaced the red cloak with a Union Flag cloak. One exception to this was unveiled in Los Angeles in May 1999 when the lady was replaced by a prone Mike Myers, the star of the James Bond-spoof film *Austin Powers: The Spy Who Shagged Me* on Boeing 747-408, G-VTOP. The name 'Virginia Plain' was also replaced with the slogan 'Austin Powered'. A figure of $300,000 was rumoured to have been paid to the airline to promote the film. (*Author*)

Western Pacific

Western Pacific began operations on 28 April 1995 and enjoyed a short but colourful career until 4 February 1998, flying what must have been the most flamboyantly decorated fleet of aircraft that has ever existed. Many of these appeared in my earlier book *Dream Schemes* but the later logojets were every bit as colourful as their earlier contemporaries. All the aircraft in the WestPac fleet were Boeing 737-300 models, which were ideally suited to wear their sponsor's colours. The 'Crested Butte, Gunniston, Colorado' scheme was unveiled in December 1996, initially as N509AU, and later became N953WP. Previously it had worn the 'WestPac Willie' scheme. Both sides of the aircraft showed different recreational aspects of the area, with the starboard side depicting a skier and snow-covered mountain, while the port side featured an angler catching a large fish. Following WestPac's collapse the aircraft went to America West where it was re-registered N332AW. (*Author's collection*)

Another aircraft in the WestPac fleet also promoted a local resort, in this case the location was the Purgatory Resort, Durango, Colorado. Rolled out on 17 October 1996, this aircraft also featured a different design on each side, with the port side featuring the Durango and Silverton Narrow-Gauge Railroad on the tail, while the fuselage showed the Anasazi cliff-dwellings in the Mesa Verde National Park. The starboard side featured a skier with snow-capped mountains running along the length of the fuselage. This aircraft has spent all of its life with airlines in North and South America, having been delivered to the Canadian airline CP Air in 1985 before moving to the Brazilian airline VASP. A short spell with Markair in Canada followed before it joined the WestPac fleet. It now operates with Southwest Airlines as N659SW. (*Exavia*)

The Boyd Gaming Corporation took three WestPac aircraft to operate as flying billboards for its gaming casinos, the first being for the Stardust Casino, featuring the showgirl 'Oki' on the tail. The second, Boeing 737-3Y0, N955WP, was rolled out on 29 May 1996, in an all-gold scheme promoting the Sam's Town casinos in Las Vegas, Kansas City and Tunica. A different girl was featured on each side of the tail. N955WP came to WestPac from the Venezuelan airline Avensa and now flies in the blue beachball colours of Sterling Airlines as OY-SEE. (*Exavia*)

The third logojet for the Boyd Gaming Corporation, N956WP, which also promoted the Sam's Town casinos in Las Vegas, Kansas City and Tunica, wore a similar all-gold scheme. Prior to appearing in these colours the aircraft flew in an all-metal finish (why waste paint when there's a sponsor in the pipeline to pay for the painting for you?) and the titles 'Future Sam's Town Jet'. In June 1997 WestPac announced that it was to merge with the Denver-based Frontier Airlines, another 737 user and only sixty miles north of WestPac's base in Colorado Springs. This proposed merger was short-lived, however, and on 6 October 1997, Western Pacific filed for Chapter 11 bankruptcy. A package was forthcoming from a New York financing organisation, to the tune of $50 million, released in stages, which should have helped the airline emerge from its bankruptcy. Sadly this was not enough to revive its fortunes and on 4 February 1998, the airline ceased operations. (*Author's collection*)